My Name Is Romero

""Ni de aquí, ni de allá" (not from here, not from there) is a saying and a dynamic that many of us Latinx/Chicano/Hispanic people struggle with. David tackles this theme and the complexities of how this mindset effects not only the personal, but also our role, or perceived roles, in modern America."

—Ulises Bella, multi-instrumentalist, founding member of Ozomatli

Some Latino poets like Willie Perdomo dish out the grit of living on the margins with superb poetical musical cadence in his 2014 *The Essential Hits of Shorty Bon Bon: Poems*. Other writers like Daniel Borzutzky – a 2016 National Book Award Winner for *The Performance of Becoming Human* – immortalize the monumental horror of terror and torture of being "Othered." What makes Romero's book *My Name Is Romero* a good addition to the Latin@/x canon is the honesty of the subject matter. The title of the book is not simply what it implies – the centering of the "Self" – of one Latino. Instead, it's an informed, intrepid, and at times, painful revelation of thoughts and dialogue that lie unspoken in our brains and amongst many Latin@/xs, and in Latin@/x communities.

—Yolanda Nieves, associate professor at Wilbur Wright College, founder of Vida Bella Ensemble

"*My Name Is Romero* is David A. Romero's open letter to the world, excavating his personal history while explicating his identity. Comprised of poems that are both deeply contemplative and astutely hilarious, Romero uncovers both the etymology of his name and what it means to really know who you are. In poem after poem he asks, "if you don't know where you come from / how're you supposed to know where you're going?" Romero knows both and with these poems he offers an empowering map for his readers to liberate themselves and stake their claim."

—Mike "The Poet" Sonksen author of *Letters to My City* and *I Am Alive in Los Angeles*

"*My Name Is Romero* is so rich and layered! Romero has so many ideas flowing!"

—Ana Maria Alvarez, founding artistic director of CONTRA-TIEMPO urban Latin dance theater company

My Name Is Romero

by

David A. Romero

Cover art by

Sonia Romero

FLOWERSONG
PRESS

FLOWERSONG

P R E S S

FlowerSong Press

McAllen, Texas 78501

Copyright © 2020 by David A Romero

ISBN: 978-1-7345617-6-0

Published by FlowerSong Press
in the United States of America.
www.flowersongpress.com

Set in Adobe Garamond Pro

Cover art by Sonia Romero. soniaromero.net

Typeset by Matthew Revert matthewrevert.com

"Open Letter to Katt Williams" first published in *Heartfire: Revolutionary Poets Brigade Anthology (Volume 2)*, Kallatumba Press. 2013. "Letters Across Borders" first published in *The Border Crossed Us – An Anthology to End Apartheid*, VAGABOND. 2015. "Temecula" first published in *Revolutionary Poets Brigade - Los Angeles*, VAGABOND. 2014.

"Sweet Pochx Pie" published in *Brooklyn & Boyle*. July 2013.

"Gorilla Arms" first published in *Label Me Latina/o* Spring 2014 Volume IV. "Open Letter to Edward James Olmos" published on *Latino Rebels*. "Undocumented Football," "Open Letter to Edward James Olmos," "Sweet Pocho Pie," and "The Ladder – For Anastasio Hernandez-Rojas," published on *La Bloga*. "Make Me More Mexican," "Sweet Pochx Pie," and "Open Letter to Edward James Olmos" published on *Poets Responding to SB1070*.

This book is dedicated to my grandparents
Delia & Edward Romero
1939

Table of contents

My Name Is...

Flowers

Beloved

Etymology

Ny Name Is Romero

Introduction

No one's story is merely their own. When someone meets you for the first time, they are more likely to ask if you have any brothers or sisters, or where your parents are from, than to ask you what your favorite color is, or what song you'd like to have played at your funeral. We feel like we can understand a person by learning about their family. We are all part of family lines that are much, much, larger than ourselves and stretch hundreds of years into the past. Knowledge of who, and what, has come before, can be both a blessing and a curse.

Before I had any idea what my name meant, others were trying to define it for me. My first memories of my last name stretch back to elementary school, and kids, who, obviously had never actually read Shakespeare's *Romeo and Juliet*, who called me "Romeo." Instead, they were intentionally mispronouncing my name to make fun of me. However, I would notice over the years, that there were lots of people who weren't deliberately trying to ridicule my surname but mispronounced it regardless. They called me "Romeo" too.

Whether as "Romeo," or "Romero," people tended to think I was Italian. Telling them that my last name was Spanish, and the reason it was Spanish was because I was Mexican, didn't settle the issue. With it came more questions. Why didn't I "look Mexican?" Why didn't I "act Mexican?" Why didn't I speak Spanish? These were all questions stemming from preconceived notions of Mexican and Latinx identity. As a young man, I had a hard time understanding these ideas myself, let alone, was I ready to answer questions and take on challengers. They're questions that I'm asked to this day, and even now, I can't convince some people to overcome their initial confusion and disbelief.

When I noticed the way that my uncle, artist Frank Romero, signed his paintings and saw his signature on walls in galleries and in books, for the first time, I became convinced that the name Romero really meant something. Having the name Romero was no longer simply being a Mexican outsider in a mostly white and Asian neighborhood. In some parts of Los Angeles, having the last name Romero was the key to a world of art, culture, and history. For many, it was a callback to the 1960s and the Chicanx Movement.

While some kids are taken by their parents to amusement parks on the other side of the country or go with them on tropical cruises, our family vacations consisted of my father loading up our van and driving us on road trips to either visit relatives, Catholic holy sites (for my mom), or to do genealogy research. On one such trip to Santa Fe, New Mexico, we did all three. We stopped at libraries as well as Catholic and LDS churches (The Church of Jesus Christ of Latter-Day Saints keeps excellent genealogy records). This was the first time I got a much larger sense of where my father's family had come from. It was cool to be able to chart our family's history.

This book is an attempt to relay that history through poetry. *My Name Is…* builds up from personal struggles with identity to expressions of Mexican pride, Latinidad, as well as calls for solidarity with other peoples. *Flowers*, the Greek translation of "Anthony" (the middle name that my father and I share), deals with people, both fictional and those based on historical figures, who lived through times of great upheaval and were caught in the machinations of various rulers. *Beloved*, the Hebrew translation of "David," is about a few ex-girlfriends. *Etymology* is a single poem providing a meaning for the name Romero by placing it within a genealogical context. For *Etymology*, it was my original intent to supplement the poem with genealogical charts documenting as much of our family lines as possible, however, it occurred to me that by making the various political statements I am making in this book, it would be unwise to include the various names and faces of my family members as they might object to those statements, and/or it might compromise their safety and the safety of their friends and families.

My stage name, David A. Romero, is my real name. However, it is an intentional inclusion of my middle initial, and not the full, "Anthony." It is meant to call attention to the fact that I am just one of many Romeros.

Our family is just one of many lines. This is not the story of each one of us. Far from it. Still, let it be a call for every Romero to proclaim pride in their name.

Hopefully one day I'll be able to afford to have some children. In the meantime, here's another book.

Sincerely,

david A Romero

David A. Romero
2020

P.S. Romero means "rosemary" (as in, the herb, not the woman with the infamous baby).

P.S.S. Yes, it *is* proper to capitalize the word "is" in titles, such as My *Name Is Romero.* Look it up.

My Name Is...

My Name Is Romero

It happens
Every
Single
Night
Telemarketing Juliets
Calling from their ivy-covered balconies
Calling for their star-crossed lovers
Calling,
"Hello"
"Is Mr. Romeo in?"
I'm sorry
Romeo went to go grab a burrito
Mercutio to cruise Whittier Boulevard
And Shakespeare to take some ethnic studies classes
In other words…
Romeo isn't in!
My name is Romero!
I am not Italian
Spanish blood
Coursing through these veins
Though my parents are not from Spain
And despite the Southern Californian accent
That allows words like
"Dude"
"Sweet"
And "sick"
To tumble gracefully from these lips
I'm not a white guy!
I'm a Mexican!

My name is Romero!
Romero like Archbishop Oscar Romero
Zombie filmmaker George A. Romero
Actor
Cesar Romero
Yes!
Before
Jack Nicholson
Before
Heath Ledger
A brown man
Played the Joker
They dressed him up in green wig
Purple suit
And white face
Though he would not shave
His trademark suave
And sexy
Latin mustache
No!
He was a Romero!
I am a Romero!
My parents had dark skin
And dark eyes
When I was seven
My brother lied
Told me my father
Was the mailman
"How could you be the son of our parents
With your blue eyes
And white skin?"

Well, brother
Like Jerry Springer or Maury
The DNA results are in!
I am a Romero!
And I know what some of you are thinking
That I'm just another white guy
Trying to prove he's a Latino
Or just another Mexican
Chest-beating
Beating his chest
Beating whatever reputation he has left
Trying to convince you
That his family
His country
His nationality
Are better
Than you!
Well
I know as well as anyone
That we are all the children of Africa
Roots of no single family tree
But of a flourishing forest
That grows majestically
Towards a magnificent destiny
Shining
Radiating beauty
Just please
Close your eyes
And you can see it…
But the name of this poem isn't,
"We are the world"

"We are the children"
No!
The name of this poem
Is "My Name Is Romero!"
Because if you're not proud of who you are
Then what're you gonna be proud of?
And if you don't know where you come from
How're you supposed to know where you're going?
And I know one thing:
That the name of my father
And my father's father
And his father's father
Before him
Was Romero.

Undocumented Football

When life throws everything at you
Don't drop the ball
"Don't drop the ball"
"Blue
42
Set
Hike!"
A brown quarterback's fingers
Tighten around the white laces
Of a football
Roosevelt vs. Garfield
They meet today
Upon an annual battleground
Where local legends
Spell rivalry
In defensive and offensive formations
Upon this old field
In this dirty stadium
Football sounds a lot like
Boyle Heights
Like East L.A.
Like years of pride and history
"Sounds like Roosevelt is in motion
Number 42
Miguel
Is with them
Crossing the line of scrimmage
Clad in red and yellow
His muscles tell a story"

Miguel has always been running
Running from la migra
Las placas
Everyone who wants to
Stop him
Ask him,
"¿Dónde están sus papeles?"
Where are your papers?
Miguel's too fast though
How fast?
Too fast
Too fast for borders
Laws
Checkpoints
Dogs
Too fast for fences
Ditches
Detention centers
And walls
Definitely too fast for the fool
Unfortunate enough to be D'ing up on him now
Through it all
Under the glare of stadium lights
Past the cheering
Booing
Chanting
And screaming
Through a maze of players
Like a beam of holy light
Miguel's vision is clear
He loves this game

It gives him focus
Gave him purpose
Miguel will be defined by this moment
He knows this
No college will recruit him
His record doesn't really scream "draft pick"
But that's not the issue
Miguel never cared for politics
He just loved his coach
His team
This American game of football
His dream
To make a catch
In the only important game that he could
Miguel will not score the winning touchdown
This game will be added to a losing record
That will make for a losing season
There are so many reasons
For Miguel to drop the ball
Walk out of this stadium just another statistic
Undocumented student
Faceless
Immigrant
There are so many reasons for Miguel to drop the ball
So, as it spirals towards him
Carrying the weight of a future unfathomable
He repeats to himself like a prayer,
"Don't drop the ball"
"Don't drop the ball"
So, "He catches it!"
Like how he catches his diploma!

Like how he catches his degree!
Like how he catches the hand of his high school sweetheart
And they cross the threshold of that goal line together!
He cradles the ball in his arms!
Like his son John!
First born legal
First born free
To pursue his dreams
And not always be running
So damned
Hard
This is just one story from the East L.A. Classic
Roosevelt vs. Garfield
Just one game for Miguel
Of undocumented
Football.

Make Me More Mexican

¡Hola!

¿Cómo estás?

Me llamo David

Yo no hablo español

Un poquito

I will grow as paranoid

As any gringo

Or gabacho

Over Spanish spoken

The Spanish I can't understand

Escúchela

Y comprende

Es la palabra verdad

Es la lengua del pueblo?

Es la lengua de la Mexica?

Hold your tongue

Do not think to criticize me

For speaking English

When you, too

So proudly speak the language

Of your European rapists and conquerors:

Spanish

Now

Tell me who's brainwashed?

Whitewashed?

¿No hablo español?

Come back to me

When your tongue can hold words

In the ancient language of the Mexica

Nahuatl
Oh no!
This poet does spit in Nahuatl!
Now what?
Keepin' it realer than real
More authentic than authentic
Looks like we're at a Mexican standoff
Well
There may be fifty ways
Of saying,
"Snow"
In Inuit
But, all of them describe the same substance
Meaning
There are truths that can be described in any language
Make me more Mexican
A simple statement
A declaration
A cry for help!
I heard they were performing the procedure
Somewhere in a dilapidated warehouse in Tijuana!
It involves infusions of chile
Gargling mole
Consuming peyote-infused-Chiclets!
Classes on how to sell oranges
Be priests!
Architects!
And presidents!
Cops and convicts!
Sinners and saints!
It involves baptisms

In dirty sinks
Filled with salvation
And Jarritos
Splashes of Tapatio
Baptizing your tongue
Para la lengua
To spit
Fiery words
¡Chingón!
¡Chingada madre!
These words
Are whole and holy
Spoken in backyards and barbecues
Weddings and quinceañeras
Yo no hablo español
Un poquito
Make me more Mexican
Indigenous
And genuine
Halo my head
In smoke trails of sage
Take me to sit
At the feet of the pyramids
So that these visions of me
As sore-thumbed
Pink-skinned
Loin-clothed
Sunburnt
Indian
Praying to the four winds
Won't seem so shallow

And ridiculous
Yo!
No!
I dedicate this
To the temple of fútbol
With an entrance shaped like a
G-O-O-O-O-O-O-O-O-O-L
Post
Raiders and Dodgers jerseys
Cholos and cholitas
Rebels and rockers
Borders and bullets
Spanish and resistance
This
Is what makes a Mexican
And this is what doesn't
Stereotype and reality
Truth and contradiction
Sound
Fury
Quiet moments
This…
Is what makes a Mexican
Like speaking Spanish
I will learn
To make myself more Mexican
What do I want?
To have an identity
What do I want?
To feel accepted
¿Quando?

¡Ahora!
¿Dónde?
¡Aquí!
Right here
And right now.

Pardon My French

C'est la vie!
L'homme est condamné
D'être libre
Excusez-moi
Pardon my French
Some things
Just can't be translated
Une femme est une femme
A woman is a woman
And a man is a man
But the words of a foreign language
Aren't just words
They are images
Thoughts
Feelings
Pardon my insecurity
In high school
I took French instead of Spanish
Got A's in my classes
Wanting to French my French teacher
Ooo la la!
Je ne sais pas
I should've known
I should've learned
The language I was born to speak
Like a mute refusing to sign
Or a blind person
Who had never rested their fingertips across Braille
My tongue never became familiar

With the words
With the sounds
Instead
I learned French
Oui, je parle Français
I speak French
The language of love
A foreign tongue
A dead tongue
A language nobody here speaks
A love of a place
La France, Paris
L'architecture
L'arte
Albert Camus
Pepé Le Pew
Et Jean-Paul Sartre
But when I close my eyes
Édith Piaf fills my ears
Oil paints the color of rose
Grey rivers
Sepia skies
Weathered people
Qui mange du pain
Et boi du vin
Par la Seine
Toasting
To the red wine of life!
Mademoiselle
Vous êtes trop belle
Pour les mots je poudrai dire…

Pour les mots je poudrai écrire …
Comme la mer
Comme les montagnes
Comme les étoiles
Vous êtes …
Mais, les ananas
Ne parlent pas!
Pineapples don't speak
And Paris doesn't exist
Well, not for me
Pardon my ignorance
In high school
I took French
Because it seemed like all the stupid people
Were taking Spanish
And I wanted to be different
Like the brutally colonized of Algeria
So eloquently speaking
French
Spanish
Seemed like the backside of a Latin coin
Never to turn up
And I
Wanted to get ahead
Pardon my cowardice
But you were here last year
Remember?
I need you to remember
When you were speaking a language
But it wasn't just a language
Someone else was speaking it

And it was a secret

Casse-toi

Ta gueule

Merde

Salope

Poutain

Mademoiselles

Monsieurs

Et madames

Pardon my French.

That's a Wrap / Ode to the Burrito

"OMG

I've got the greatest idea!

We'll take the pride of your people

The most significant dish

Your culture has ever produced

And we'll turn it into

A sandwich

No, a salad

Nah, a hamburger!

No

No

No

I've got it!

We'll throw it all

On top

Of a doughy

Flour

Tortilla

And just…

Wrap it up!"

Ah

Hell

No

The seventh seal

Was broken

The seventh trumpet

Was sounded

And from the seas arose

A dark and unholy beast

Its name
Featured on fast food menus
And neon signs
All over the country…
The wrap
The focus group of foods
You were assembled
From the rotting carcasses of recipes
Killed by cultural appropriation
You are a Frankenstein
A monster
And for those travelers
Who journeyed
Throughout Mexico and the Southwest
On burros
Who invented the burrito
The little donkey
You are truly an ass!
Scraps of better foods
Whose quality was sacrificed
At the unholy altar of
"On the go"
You are simultaneously
Warm chicken
And cool salad
You are lukewarm
I will spit you out and reject you
As they reject us
Those who want cash in on the popularity of the burrito
But deny Spanish from the menu?
Those who love Mexican food

But hate Mexicans.
And what have we given
To the world?
The burrito
Is a pillow
For your mouth!
It is a voluptuous breast
A full butt cheek
And only for the poor in spirit
Is there something threatening
About its size!
It is pollo
Carnitas
Carne asada
And not ground beef
With
Or without
A side of beans and rice
Guacamole please
But no pinche sour cream!
The burrito
Is quite simply
An essay on humanity's struggle
For greatness
Greatness achieved!
A burrito is all the things that a wrap is not
Ban wraps forever!
Burn all images that carry their name and likeness in effigy!
And on that brave new day
You'll find me
At Manuel's El Tepeyac

In Boyle Heights, Los Angeles
Eating a burrito
As big
As your head.

THE END.

Sweet Pochx Pie

I'm as American
As sweet pochx pie
Light flaky crust
Identity crisis inside
Like apples to oranges
We are pochxs
Children of these lands claimed
Ambassadors to a great American immigration
That often doesn't want us
Our ancestors were criminalized
For speaking Spanish
Yet, we're expected to speak it
Flawlessly
Without an accent
Expected to fit a stereotypical appearance
While Spanish language TV stations display the opposite
Ask someone on a Latinx panel how to succeed in America
They will answer,
"Remember:
You're a professional first
Latinx second"
As if the two were mutually exclusive!
Pochxs pronounce our last names wrong
Argue this has become right
As my name is Romero
Becomes my name is "ROW-MARROW!"
And rolling R's seem as silly to me
As caricatures of twirling mustaches
When saying my own name properly

Makes me feel like Zorro
Like Detroit Red
Becoming Malcolm X
Or like a boy named Sue
With something to prove
Pochxs can make for the best of activists
Carrying chips on our shoulders
The size of boulders
Emblazoned scrolls upon these read
"Doubt"
"Shame"
"Guilt"
Enough for late nights
And long marches
To connect with the people
Ambassadors to a great American immigration
That often doesn't want us
Teases us bare and naked
Points out
How tenuous
Our relationship to being Latinx is
How it so easily crumbles…
Like a light
Flaky
Crust
More apple than orange
Sweet pochx pie
"Sold out" here
"¡Gringo! ¡Gringa! ¡Gringx!"
They cry
Some pochxs are sliced

Into a permanent state of denial
Cut themselves
"White"
Or "Other"
For pie charts
Others go on a journey of discovery of their Latinx roots
With all the subtlety and discretion of Christopher Columbus
Leaving division and destruction in their wake
Crushed hopes
Broken dreams
Promises of a piece of the pie with nothing inside
That's why some in our communities fear us
Who are we?
The pochxs you didn't want
The pochxs you taunt
For trying to be everything to everyone
We laugh, dance, scream, sing, argue, and smile
We taste sweet as pochx pie
Smell the air
Look at the crowd
Feast upon their eyes
America loves
Sweet pochx pie.

Gorilla Arms

It was Sunday morning
My father
Had just gotten off work
Overtime shift
Family room
Pink box of donuts
My father's blue work shirt
That put them on the table
Exhausted
But happy
Spending time with the family
His arms on the table
Muscular
Sweaty
Heavy
Hairy
Arms
A bratty
Snotty-nosed child
I looked across the table
And told him,
"You look like a gorilla"
It wasn't just the words
It was the cock of the head
The wrinkling of the nose
The arch of the eyebrow
It wasn't just the words
It was the sneer
Tucked inside of them

"You look like a gorilla"
Who was this stranger
Who lived in my house?
Spent hours tinkering in the garage
Or lumbering out in the yard
Yelled to rake up the leaves
Pick up the dog poop
Mow the lawn
Left before I went to school
Left in the middle of the night
Oftentimes, returned the same
Always wearing that blue or orange uniform
Always tired
On those days
Prone to anger
Big
Heavy
Work boots
Clonking and clomping
Throughout the house
Sometimes he was covered in dirt
His hair uncombed and wild
Work shirt unbuttoned
Chest hair out
Hairy arms
Like gorilla sleeves
Who was this stranger?
He was my dad
My father
"You look like a gorilla"
It wasn't just the words

It was the inflection
It was my reflection
It was the teachers
The guest lecturers
The people on television
The parents of my friends
No one had ever told me
That I should
Want to be like my father
Blue-collar
Work with your hands
Muscular
Sweaty
Heavy
Hairy
Arms
He used them
To clean ditches
Build pipe systems
To cut down trees
To clear fields
And embankments
Every day
For us
"You look like a gorilla"
There was hate there
Disgust there
Dehumanization
Like how Creationists can find nothing more filthy
Than to say that humans
Are descended from monkeys

(Chimpanzees)
Like how racists call Mexicans "cockroaches"
Cackle when they hear "La Cucaracha"
The Nazis called the Jews "rats"
Blacks were depicted for decades
As more "ape"
Than homo sapient
My brother
Commented on how they treated him at work,
"They treat me like their workhorse"
A beast of burden
This was his first admission
This
Was racism
They treated him like a Mexican
And he hated it
My father
Was as stubborn as a bull
As strong as an ox
Muscular
Sweaty
Heavy
Hairy
Arms
Gorilla arms
The arms that built our house
The arms
That hugged my mother
That carried me as a child
I looked at those arms
That Sunday morning

And told him,
"You look like a gorilla"
Everything stopped
Everyone was shocked
Soon, there was shouting
Screaming
I ran
Crying
Out of the house
And into the backyard
"You look like a gorilla"
I will regret saying that
For the rest of my life.

Micro Machines

Mexican kid with the white skin and blue eyes
Knows a lot about art
This brings a smile to the white face of a museum docent
She asks the boy how he knows so much
The boy replies,
"My uncle is an artist"
The boy says this without a hint of cynicism or derision
This
To him
Is the greatest thing a person can be
An artist
The docent asks the boy,
"What's his name?"
"Frank Romero"
"What does your uncle paint?"
"Cars"
"He paints old cars"
American cars from the 1920s through 50s
L.A.
Palm trees
Freeways
And familiar streets
As the background
Always bold in color
With a zigzagged impasto stroke
The kind of thing you see that immediately makes you say,
"That's a Romero"
The boy suggests to the docent,
"Maybe he has something here?"

A pause from her, then,
"There's an auto museum down the street
Maybe he has something there"
No, that doesn't seem right...
"Maybe what you mean is - - he paints - - cars"
There's a dusty wood and tin garage under this museum
And the docent has put his uncle into it
They call this aggression
But, really, it's so easy, as she does it
But, his uncle doesn't look the same there
His uncle
With bold, striped sweaters
Full, wild hair, and beard
Laugh, big enough to fill a room
Larger than-life-personality
Looks very different in the docent's garage
To her, his uncle is a tiny uncle
With a shaved head
Brown Pendleton and Dickies
Navy work apron
And silver paint spray can in hand
He paints with that
In place of a brush
The cars in the garage
Are smaller too
They're micro machines
And like them
The boy feels small
And getting smaller
His hopes
His pride

All the world and its colors
Shrinking to a vanishing point
Because he knows what she means.

I know what she meant
I couldn't expand upon these ideas fast enough.

There is nothing wrong with painting cars
Painting pictures of cars
Or, dressing like a cholo
But, we are not all the same
You can't paint us all with the same brush
Fit us all into the same stroke
Whatever the medium
There is nothing wrong with taking pride in your work
But, what is wrong
Is for anyone to assume
That we are a smaller people
A lesser people
It is wrong to assume
That any one of us can't be acclaimed
Can't hang
In your museum
Give him the top floor
Because my uncle is an artist
A painter
His work has hung in galleries the world over
You can find him in the Smithsonian
See his mural in L.A.
By the 101
And, yes

He, like me
Is a Mexican!
My uncle is an artist
A painter
Who's been paid to paint cars
That were literally
Bigger than the Mona Lisa
My uncle is an artist
A painter
And like me he knows how to use
The principle of diminution
Which is making objects smaller in a piece of art
To help create a sense of perspective
My uncle is an artist
A painter
And he doesn't get paid to talk about paintings
He gets paid to paint them
With checks
Bigger than your desperate attempts
To try and re-frame him
And I won't let any of you
Make me feel small about any of us
Ever again.

Poor, Poor Spaniard

As "Mexicans cross the border"
And "Mexicans hop the fence"
As "Mexicans line up at Home Depot"
And the news announces
Yet "another Mexican arrest"
You tell the world
Chest out and proud,
"My family may have come from Mexico
But we
We
Are Spaniards"
Poor, poor, Spaniard
You wear your arrogance
Like steel-plated armor
Drink from glasses
With edges sharper than
The ends of conquistador helmets
I pray
As you sip
You do not cut your lips
You sit
In air-conditioned living rooms
Imagine them
As open-aired verandas
You like to show off
How light your skin is
"Blue and green eyes," you say,
"Run in the family"
The splash of color of dresses in a twirl

Dancing
Only for the right occasion
And certainly not enough
To sweat
Otherwise
They might think you were
Getting out of hand
They might think you were
GASP!
A Mexican!
Poor, poor Spaniard
How dare you fling words like,
"Wetback"
"Illegal?"
How dare you
Fill the word "Mexican"
With spite!
The ancestors you claim
Committed genocide!
Poor, poor, Spaniard
You weep for your lost land
Hold on to your claims
This charade has gone on long enough
Old and tired pieces of paper?
There is as much to them
As Don Quixote's daydreams
And the truth is a windmill
Sweeping down to knock you off your high horse
True
We Mexicans are not all
Descendants of Aztec princes and princesses

More of our ancestors
Buried beneath stone blocks
Than atop
But, yes,
The blood
It flows through veins
Eyes cannot be stopped
From wandering
Indio
Maya
Yaqui
Mulatto
Aztec
Mexica
You see your own people
And you say,
"They should go back to Mexico!"
Poor, poor, Spaniard
If you love Spain so much
Why don't you go back there?
And what will you find there?
Your sangre pura?
Nearly eight hundred years of
African and Arabic influence
Language
Architecture
Science
Moorish lute
Made Spanish guitar
Rhythmic dances
And your beloved

Spanish rice
From Egypt
Iraq
And Iran
Poor, poor, American
Something lost
Something imaginary
Is your only claim
Your allegiances shift
With the flag of the day
The melting pot
For you
Is good
Only if you make sure
You have erased the ingredients
You stay on your side of the fence
Now, you answer:
Did you come from Mexico?
Did you come from Spain?
Did you come from some white Eden
In the Middle East
Or North Africa?
Where did you come from
To keep your blood so pure
And your nose so high?
Where did you come from
To dare fill the word "Mexican" with spite?"
Show me on the map
Yes…
That's right
Nowhere

You poor, poor
Nothing.

Who Wins?

Flip on the TV
Turn on the radio
The game is on
You lazily ask,
"Who's winning?"
The Atlanta Braves
The Kansas City Chiefs
The Washington Redskins
Are playing
You change the channel
The hipsters
Are going native
With dreamcatchers hanging
Over their beds
And their rearview mirrors
They're defusing accusations of racism
By saying they're,
"1/16 Cherokee"
You can hear indigenous flutes playing in their songs
See Kokopelli welcome mats under their doors
They're running into the woods
Partying in the desert at outdoor festivals
With war paint and headdresses
Doing drugs once considered sacred
So wild and free
On top of stolen land
They're screaming and dancing
They're shrugging off questions of cultural appropriation
Getting philosophical as they get defensive,

"It feels like you're trying to start
An argument
With that
And the thing about that is
You know
Who wins?"
You change the channel
Apocalypse Now
Predator
28 Days Later
The white savior
Covers himself with mud
Strips naked
Howls into the night
Alone in the wilderness
He must plunge into the heart of darkness
To win
Our hero must go native
Change the channel
Now for something classic
Cowboys
Indians
Bows
Arrows
Feathers
Horses
Wagon trains
Gunshots
You know who will ride on
And you know who will fall
You know who wins

Change the channel
It's Pocahontas
Peter Pan
Tiger Lilly
The beautiful Native American woman
Must be won over
Saved from the evil clutches
Of the savage red man!
Change the channel
It's a documentary
It's history
Native Americans
Lose everything
They fall to disease
To genocide
To poverty
To alcoholism
To rape
First-nations peoples
Almost extinct
This kind of bums you out
So, you change the channel
It's a commercial
For a Native American casino
You like this channel
The bright lights
The polished walls of the brand-new casino
Someone says,
"Heck, they're the ones winning now!"
Turn the TV off
Do some research

15% Native American unemployment
Less than $12,000 annual Native American per capita income
Over $28 billion made in tribal gaming last year
Sounds like a big win
You know who also made a killing in America last year?
JPMorgan Chase
Wells Fargo
Exxon Mobil
How did it feel when you got a piece of those winnings?
That's right
You didn't
The tables are rigged
The house always wins
The slot machines spew broken promises
Broken treaties
With dates ranging from 1890 to 1770
These coins
They clang
They crash
The sound is deafening
Dead presidents
Pressed on metal
Printed on paper
Whose value
Is the perception of trust
If you could gather them all up
The falseness
The falsehood
The toll
The cost
The bloodshed

The heartbreak
The weight of it
The loss
Would crush you
And butcher everything that you love
Like pale horses
And buffalo
On a field of blood
In a house
With a TV set
It's the victors
Who ask,
"Who wins?"

Patriots & Lunatics

It would be a disservice
To give self-appointed patriots
Dirt and grit
Stars and stripes
Red-blooded Americans
The title "lunatic"
Except when
It fits them
As comfortably
As orange jumpsuits
Or pine box coffins
Chris Simcox
Was a man with an American dream
Move out to the Southwest
Grab some guns
Take a last stand
Like Wyatt Earp
At the O.K. Corral
Shoot it out until the bitter end
Aside from the usual delusions of grandeur
Chris Simcox
Co-founder of the Minutemen
Harbored a much darker secret.

At night
We arrive
Never me
Not I
I've never been there

When they cross
From Sonora to Arizona
Chiuahua to Texas
But I know it
Not the types to be intimidated
By a line on a map
A line in the sand
Or a river
I picture them emerging from the water
Indignant
Clothes soaked
Wet shirts and blouses
Over wet backs
They call them "wetbacks"
As if somehow
The strength in them
To carry adversity
Would be grounds
For anything derogatory
You should add
"Alerteyes"
"Callusedhands"
"Muscledtorsos"
"Sunhardenedskin"
"Tiredanddehydratedbutstillrunninglegs"
To that long list of epithets
"Wetback"
Is just another word for survivor.

"There were no survivors"
Home massacre

Jason "J.T." Ready
Neo Nazi
Former member of the Minutemen
Put a gun to his head
But not before murdering
His girlfriend
Her daughter
Her daughter's boyfriend
And their child.

Brisenia Flores
Was nine years old
When she was murdered
By the Minutemen
Shawna Forde
Jason Eugene Bush
Albert Gaxiola
Two Minutemen and their guide
Crept into the Flores house
Under the cover of night
Looking for drugs
They didn't find any
So, they shot Brisenia
Her mother
And her father
Stole their jewelry
Rode back to their hideout
Didn't make out with much
Not enough to cover the cost of a new headquarters
See, these vigilantes
Had a patriotic plan

They were going to rob them some Mexicans
To fund the training and arming of more Minutemen
Because it's Mexicans who are the dangerous ones, right?

Chris Simcox
Co-founder of the Minutemen
Has a problem
Has a disease
This defender of American values
And American children
Couldn't stop himself from touching them
Three girls
Under the age of ten
Five counts of pedophilia
Including
Acts perpetrated against his own daughter.

I am glad
That our borders
Are kept safe
By patriots
And lunatics
Dead
Or locked up for now
While more cowboys
Vigilantes
Neo Nazis
Pedophiles
Murderers
And Minutemen
Ride off into the sunset

They ride
With blood on their hands
Waiting for us
To finally
Bury them.

Open Letter to Donald Trump

Dear Donald Trump
In 2015
You announced your candidacy
For President of the United States
In front of American flags
Podium bearing your name
A platform of hate
Talked about making America great
For who?
It wasn't for us
Latinx America
You called us "criminals"
"Drug dealers"
And "rapists"
A nameless wave of people
Coming "from Mexico"
And "South America"
Donald Trump
Do you know anything?
Heard of Central America?
Thought to throw in a statistic?
Like 7% of immigrants come to America from
El Salvador, Guatemala, and Honduras?
Would saying the places we come from
The most basic of differences
Have alienated your supporters?
Yes
The suburban racists
The hardcore hicks

To them
It's too much to say
"Latinx"
"Hispanic"
Or "indigenous"
To them we're "all Mexicans"
Or we're "all spics"
Donald Trump
You call us "criminals"
Maybe you forgot
How the United States stole half of Mexico
How NAFTA stole much of what was left
Maybe you forgot about the theft
Of the lives of
Torrijos
Allende
And Arbenz
Maybe you forgot about
The bombing of Panama
And the United Fruit Company
You call us "drug dealers" Trump
Maybe you forgot about Oliver North
And his testimony about Iran-Contra
Forgot about the CIA's dealings in Nicaragua
About how they used Freeway Rick Ross
To flood crack cocaine into the ghetto
You call us "rapists" Trump
Are you speaking for the women of Juarez?
For the victims of American sex tourism?
Do you deny
That when she dared to question you

You said that Megyn Kelly must've bleeding out of her
You-know-what?
Do you deny that you've frequently made comments
About wanting to have sex
With your own daughter?
Do you deny that you continually call women
All women
And not just Rosie O'Donnell
Pigs?
Some say you're a joke Trump
But when you use a platform of hate
To become the President of the United States
I'm not laughing
Because you've made it clear
That there is a seething mass
In the heart of this country
That is deeply racist
Xenophobic
Islamophobic
Queerphobic
Misogynistic
You're no sideshow Trump
You're the main stage
The old racism
The mean racism
Back in town
We need to fight you now
Or we may never get another chance
Some say you're a joke Trump
But when you use a platform of hate
To become the President of the United States

I'm not laughing
Because I know
That when you say that we are
"Criminals"
"Drug dealers"
And "rapists"
You mean business
And so do I
Donald Trump, you are fired
Donald Trump, you should've stayed bankrupt
Should've had your tie stapled to the sewing machines
In the sweatshop factories you produce your clothes in
Should've had your casinos and tower
Collapse on top of your head
You should've suffered a stroke in your tanning bed
And let the ultra violet light slowly work its magic
Donald Trump, you should've had your hair
Caught in a freak accident
And been swung around by it like a Troll doll
Because Latinx America
Is the future America!
People of Color America
Is the future America!
And we don't take kindly
To being called "criminals"
"Drug dealers"
Or "rapists"
We're the best of the best
The majority shareholders
In 2044
Or earlier

Donald Trump
You had better hope it isn't
A hostile
Takeover.

Open Letter to Edward James Olmos

Dear Edward James Olmos
It has come to my attention
That you took a flight back from the Super Bowl
With the Governor of Arizona
Jan Brewer
I may have been deceived
Because you are such an accomplished actor
But it looks like that was your arm
Hanging over plush and white cushions
Draped over her slippery shoulders
I may have been deceived
Because you are such an accomplished actor
But it looks like you two
Are smiling like old friends
In your Instagram picture together
#edwardjamesolmos
#chicanonomore
Como se dice,
"Sellout?"
Como se dice,
"Race traitor?"
Como se dice,
"Got what he wanted
Then threw us
Under the freedom bus
Headed for Arizona?"
Sounds like Monteczuma
Feels like nostrils flaring
Feels like saliva and mocos

Gathered up in mouth
And hurled at your feet
You have betrayed us
Edward James Olmos
"Now boarding"
Could you feel something
Deep in your bones
Telling you not to get on that plane?
Stories of corpses haunting the desert
Of Minutemen patrols
Did their victims give you pause?
Could you feel something
Tugging at your heartstrings?
Those violins
Serenading
Another funeral party
Did they move you?
Could you feel something
Like a knife
Stabbing into your traitor's belly
Like you were stopped
In front
Of red
And blue lights
Flashing
Frozen in terror
Watching as they come?
Did you excuse yourself
After you took the photo?
Did you wipe the sin
Off your hands

And lose yourself
In a swirling drain of remorse?
No
¡Chale!
You felt fine
Flying high
Governor Bruja
Never gets stopped!
She flies over borders
Travels with impunity
Because she owns the law!
And besides
What's the plight of your people
When you can get an easy ride
Back from the Super Bowl?
Edward James Olmos
Chicano actor
Activist
What will you tell us?
That in that cramped airplane compartment
You maneuvered through niceties?
"Dialogued"
About
"Understanding"
And "social policy?"
Or
Will you tell us
That you cursed her
Through those smiling teeth of yours?
Is that what you did?
No!

Because that would take
¡Ganas!
Ganas you apparently left back in New Orleans!
But
If we are to tell stories
Here's one for you:
Your plane never touched down in Arizona
It was grounded
It fit a profile
Of the 1%
Politicians
And sell-outs like yourself
A loud voice boomed,
"Freeze!
We need to see your papers and ID!"
Jan Brewer was escorted from the plane
Belligerent
And brought out in handcuffs
Tried for her crimes against humanity
And you Edward James Olmos?
We stripped you of your zoot suit
Of names
We had held close to our hearts
For so many years
Adama
Santana
Escalante
El Pachuco
Edward James Olmos
All we were left with
Was your sad carcass

An empty plane
And the realization
You had never been
The first Chicano
Anything.

Open Letter to Katt Williams

Dear Katt Williams
You are not welcome in my home
Nor in the homes
Of the millions of Mexicans and Latinxs
You despise for their national pride
You will find
Reflections
Of green
White
And red
In the family restaurants of Italians
Find reflections
Of green
White
And orange
In the pubs of the American Irish
You are not welcome
By those blacks
Whites
And Asians
Who would stand with us
We all have a right to be here!
A right to celebrate were we come from!
So, may this letter find its way to your mailbox
As emails flood your inbox
Your answering machine
Overfilled with phone calls
So, that your words
Might be turned

Into something less trashy
More useful
We're going to wreck your tour schedule
Ban you from the airwaves
Remove you from Comedy Central and HBO
You have crossed the line between comedy
And being an…
So
May this letter find its way into your mailbox
Decorated
Red
White
And blue
Adorned with a leering eagle
You would claw out our eyes
Rip out our tongues
You have forgotten
That the eagle
Who adorns the flag of my people
Is well-used to killing snakes
And your tongue
Has been found
Slithering
If I saw you backstage
I would cut out your heart
Expose it
Rusty
Copper-colored
And yellow
As you bellowed,
"We were slaves, b…

Y'all just a bunch of gardeners!"
Taking off your hat
Exposing bite marks
From a swim
With a great white
Nation
I've heard of biting the hand that feeds
But you, Katt Williams?
You have been feeding the hand that bites
For
Far
Too
Long
You tell us to go home
This is our home!
Some people call our children "anchor babies"
Then
Anchors aweigh!
We're here to stay!
You were found chanting
"USA!
USA!"
In the same state
That chose not to celebrate the birthday of
MLK
MLK
You have clearly
Chosen your targets wisely
Far too easy
When you sniff power
From Jan Brewer's navel

Keep warm in tents
With Sheriff Joe Arpaio
Suck the truth
From Bill O'Reilly's lips
Take it rough
And uncut
With Glen Beck
Katt Williams
Even a pimp in parody
Becomes a prostitute
When he performs in
Phoenix,
Arizona
Where our dreams go to die
We act now
To burn this city down
And piss on its ashes
So, your nonsense
Will never rise
Again.

Black and Brown: Fight Tonight!

It's black and brown
Fight tonight
It's the fight of the century
And how many more?
The viewers at home
Have chosen their winners
Long before the first scorecard
Or ring of the bell
And in this corner
Black
African-American
By way of West Africa
Transatlantic slave trade
From American plantations
To the first private prison
From the prisons to the fields
Fields to the factories
Factories to unemployment
Unemployment to poverty
The inner city
Smoldering
Almost no way out
But
Sports
Conditioning
Fists
Flying
And in this corner
Brown

Chicanx
By way of Mexico
New Spain
Aztec Empire
Before the Spaniards came
Pushed off the land
And into the barrio
The barrio
Smoldering
Almost no way out
But
Sports
Conditioning
Fists
Flying
From all of Latin America
It is the same
They fight
Black and brown
Touch gloves
Let's get ready for battle!
And here it goes
The racist jokes
Each individual fighter
Now longer themselves
But
A symbol
A battle between countries
Between races
Brought to you by
"They're not like us!"

"They're stealing our jobs!"
"They're kicking us out of the neighborhood!"
"They don't appreciate what they have!"
"They don't appreciate what they were given!"
"They will work for anything!"
But back to the tale of the tape
Black and brown
AGE
At least 50,000 years old
HEIGHT
Enough to stand on tippy-toes
Dream of better tomorrows
REACH
Enough to bring communities
Pull entire puzzle-pieced continents together
WEIGHT
Enough to carry these smoldering cities
Upon our backs
Our lives
Just as heavy
If we're in the same class…
When your time to fight comes
Fight for black and brown unity
Because this fight
Spills out of the ring
Onto the jobsite
Into our homes
Into the schools
With fists
Flying
Knives

Thrusting
Cartridges
Emptying
Ambulances
Arriving
Bodybags
Filling
And chock outlines that remain
Long
After the
Final
Knockout.

Watch the Throne

Jay-Z and Kanye West
Weren't kidding when they said,
"Watch the throne"
Pretenders and usurpers abound
Looking to steal the crown
From LA to Tokyo
You already know
America will have its next Great White Hope
Even if it has to be imported
I don't care how "Fancy" these emcees get
Hip Hop and American music
Have always been
Black
In the 1920s
Paul Whiteman
Ordained the first "King of Jazz"
His scepter?
A cane
His cape?
A long-tailed coat
His crown?
A top hat
His subjects?
The American press
His sound?
Whiter than his name
Paul Whiteman
Just like

Nick LaRocca
First jazz band leader ever recorded
Claimed he had invented the music
After hearing it
Playing on the keys
Of the pianos
Of the bars in Storyville
Or was it blaring
From the horns of those saints
Marching with Louis Armstrong?
In the 1930s
Benny Goodman
"The King of Swing"
Elvis
"The King of Rock n' Roll"
Or, simply, "The King"
But Mos Def sang,
"Elvis Presley ain't got no soul
Chuck Berry is Rock n' Roll
You may dig on the Rolling Stones
But they didn't come up with that style on they own"
Neither did the Beatles
It came in the 40s
From Louis Jordan and his Jump Blues
Sister Rosetta Tharpe
Shouting from the church pew
From the expert guitar timing of Goree Carter
"Rock Awhile"
The hours weren't counted until
Bill Haley

Sang,
"Rock Around the Clock"
Whiteman
Goodman
Presley
LaRocca
Haley
So, so many kings
Lorde wasn't kidding
When she sang,
"We could be royals
Royals"
White musicians
Have been
Royal
In Black music
For quite some time
It should come as no surprise
That Blacks had to settle for lesser titles
The Count
Basie
The Duke
Of Earl
Or Ellington
Settling for the honorable mention
Like Kendrick Lamar
Losing to Macklemore
"Best Rap Album 2014"
But when you ride with B.B. King
It is you who pull shotgun

Even if you're Eric Clapton
Maybe that's why Eminem asked,
"Why be a king?
When you can be a god?"
Well…
Michael Jackson
Is still the undisputed
"King of Pop"
Like Tupac
And Biggie
Producing albums
From beyond the grave
Ella Fitzgerald
"The Queen of Jazz"
Aretha Franklin
"The Queen of Soul"
James Brown
"The King of Soul"
Ms. Lauryn Hill
Never given her title
The throne up for grabs
Each article
Each award
Each record sale
Is theft
There is no such thing as post-racial music
In a post-racial America
There is truth
There is history
A line of succession

And there is robbery
Kings and Queens
Who will be next to sit?
Watch the throne.

Letters Across Borders

Dear US,

I've noticed
You've been putting up a lot of walls lately
We used to be close
Partners.

Dear Israel,

I've noticed
You've been putting up a lot of walls lately
We used to be close
My child.

Dear US,

We were born in fire and blood
Screaming for "Independence!"
From oppressive progenitors
In a new world
I was 300 years
In the belly of the beast
You?
Nearly 200
But our fates
Like my liberation from Maximilian
And the decision of your Civil War
Are connected.

Dear Israel,

I am very, very old
But I can still remember
How you twice roamed my deserts
First, as lost and lonely infant
Your birth name meant "those who pass over"
"Nomads"
"Wanderers"
I did not raise you easy
Kept you moving
Like my other children
I raised you to be a survivor.

Dear US,

All of these battles
These horses and cannons
The bloody war between us
Are merely the imprints of tiny feet
Leaving scars upon our bodies.

Dear Israel,

You returned from Egypt
Confident yet desperate
Eager to drink from my wells
I gave you the open desert
You wanted to build walls
But the Romans still knew you as my child.

Dear US,

Our relationship is timeless
For millennia
We have been connected
We have danced our dance
In inseparable embrace
Upon continental plates
Shifting the oceans
But not us
We are one.

Dear Israel,

You fled to Europe
Came back in sadness
I offered you my wells
Greeted you with open deserts
You had returned to build walls.

Dear US,

We now carry two names
We carry these fences
These walls
This border.

Dear Israel,

You wage war with your brothers
Push forward your borders

You deny my name
My child
My poor lost Hebrew
My poor lost Israel
You have a home now
Built atop corpses and conquest
A home of checkpoints and fences
Built atop the womb
From which I gave birth to you.

Dear US,

It's like you're trying to forget
All that we've meant to each other
I know now
That you created NAFTA
To take
And take
Without giving anything back in return.

Dear Israel,

You remain as lost
As you ever have been
Your heart is still afraid
It is still wandering
I fear for us
I fear for you.

Dear US,

You put up these walls
You build up your walls
My ear is pressed against your chest
I wonder when
I will once again
Feel your heart's beat?

Dear US & Israel,

We do not ask you to leave each other
Only that you please return to us.

Sincerely,

Mexico & Palestine

Could We Eat Our Way to World Peace?

If the moon is made of cheese
We all have plenty to eat
If we are
What we eat
What can we eat
To be peace-full?
What does peace taste like?
Does it tingle on the tongue?
Does it settle in the belly?
People have been talking about peace for years
And I'd like to give it a chance
Do they give out samples?
Is it possible?
Could we eat
Our way to world peace?

Cous cous is on the loose!
Call a truce!
Carne asada and kimchi
Oranges for Somali pirates
Matzah balls for the anti-Semite
Collard greens for the soul
We'll keep feeding hummus to the Zionist
And the Christian fundamentalist
Curry to carry us to a better tomorrow
We are changing diets
To win hearts and minds
Under the upper crust

Our world is full of ingredients
Bubbling up underneath the surface
No one here
Was meant to go hungry
Today
There will be no swollen bellies
No shirt? No shoes?
Thank you for your service!
Fill yourselves up
Let's turn the tables
So we can set them right
For the first time
Load up your shopping carts
We want you
To look at the aisles of the market
As shelves in your cabinet
Enough with equal opportunity
We want equal access
The harvest belongs
To those who grow it
Fruits
Vegetables
Amber waves of grain
This bread was meant for you
Campesino!
Surviving on pennies
Made back-broken
Central Valley
In the sun
For you
African-American!

Blamed for all
Ancestors filled the coffers of this country
Forced to pick cotton
For you
Who fight terminator seeds
Need stolen water returned
And dirty water cleaned!
This bread was meant for you!
Farmers
Who grow
Potatoes
Corn
Beans
And rice
Multinationals flood markets
Selling the same food
To customers at a lower price
They wonder
Why you would lose your land
Migrate to the city
They wonder
Why you would riot over food
This is the grapes of wrath
The wrath of grapes
This bread was meant for you
Dispossessed farmer
For you
Co-op grower
And for you
Fast food worker
You are all hungry for peace

We are all hungry for peace!
We are hungry for the sword
Not to cut us apart
Not to carve up the feast
Because the problem with the world
Is not
That we do not all hunger for peace
Or that there isn't enough
To go around
But that most of us
Were never meant
To have any on our plates
So, here's a message to you
That's our food
You drooling gluttons!
Fork it over!

Temecula

"That summer we drank heartily
To the end of all things
We swore we would stop the party
Once we had finished our glasses
Problem is, they never seemed to empty."
This is the tale of a man who crashed a party
That stretched a whole community
In a land of make-believe
In a city that never existed
In a country called America
Where manor gave way to mansion
No mention was given to impending evictions
Notices declared too ugly a decoration
For grand arches, brick and white façade
Not to match with red carpets
To reach across and litter doorstops
And behind them
Where fences and walls in backyards
Were torn down one day
For wooden tables of elegant tablecloth
To extend into horizons
Stacked with jugs and aged bottles alike
Crisp crackers and foreign cheeses
The residents chased each other like children
Fraying the fabrics of faux designer garments
Unbuttoned tuxedos and satin dresses
Screams of pleasure
Catching the glints of sunlight in swirl
Artificial turf below a field of broken sprinklers

Over imported rocks
Landscaped pools long gone dry
Fountains flowing in abundance with wine
When thirsty, no need for a waterfall
Close to angels with cup and mouth
No one can seem to remember
Who started this party
But everyone knows who supplies it
The deliverer of the elixir
A cure for worry
He, of beggary and old money
He, of sophistication and scandal
He, who wakes in piles of hay
And plush bedrooms
He of the dog that bit him
Coat tinged in mud
Lord of flies and fleas
Of bonfires
And vanity
The ring leader
Leads them into circles
With riddles to invent
Wisdom to give
Fingers to wave
Life lessons to never find their owners
Stories to tell of greatness past
Hyperbole of greatness to be,
"This city with future
As bright as afternoon light
Upon our broken chandeliers can be"
His way with words finds its way into echoes

Like the sound of silver spoon upon glass,
"Here, here
We, of the dream
We, who live beyond means
We, who thirst
And drink from golden streams
Our summer
This summer
Will never dry."
He speaks
An American of dark hair
And worn, sunburnt face
He, who this place has claimed
This man named Temecula
Was of the greatest awareness
This party could never last
In wine country
Or any other
He finishes,
"Our glasses never seemed to empty...
I knew what was coming
It was sobering
Yet, here, there and everywhere
Were wine glasses
And not to devoid them of purpose
I was of mind to fill them."
This summer was good for his sweet sayings
Good for them
Patrons of escape
In a land of make-believe
In a city that never existed

In a country called America.

The Ladder

For Antastasio Hernandez-Rojas

Tijuana
Is a ladder
San Diego
Is a ladder
My name is Anastasio
I know all about climbing ladders
I'm a painter
A roofer
They tell me
Coyotes or police
One day
I will fall off
In screams and shadow
Crash
In bones and blood
I smile
You'll only fall
If you look down
Will only look down
If you're too afraid
To climb
I've never been afraid
I know all about climbing ladders
I'm a painter
A roofer
This life is a ladder
Tijuana is a ladder
The desert is a rung

Parched lips are a rung
Dry throat is a rung
Blistered feet are a rung
Then
Hours waiting for work are a rung
The bosses are a rung
Cheap pay is a rung
ICE
La migra
La policia
Rungs
But between the aluminum
Is a view
Each view
More beautiful
Than the one before it
My kids go to college
They find work
In the shade
Never having to spend a day
Climbing ladders in the sun
I buy my wife a car
It runs
A new washing machine
A dryer
They run
Ours
For the first time
My wife
Every child
Under one roof

They run around this house
This freshly painted house
It shines like the afternoon
It rests
At the top of the ladder
I can see it
I can breathe it
I can taste it
Like when I rise from my work
And rest on my haunches
Look out over a roof
See the tiles fitting
Near completion
A glass jar of money
Almost full
I can see it
The border is a ladder
And I am getting closer
With each job
Each crossing
Even at night
I will climb
My hands will grasp each rung
Because I
Have to
Because I
Am almost there
My hands
"Hands up!"
Grasp air
"Hands up!"

I fall
"Hands up!"
My hands reach out
"Hands up!"
They surround
On the desert floor
More than a dozen
Black uniforms
Shouting figures
Malevolent faces
Illuminated by the glow of tasers
Striking like rattlesnakes
They sting and bite
I cringe and cry
Each kick is a rung
Each baton is a rung
Each kick is a rung
Each baton is a rung
Each kick is a rung
Each baton is a rung
So many, many rungs
The light from the house fades
Somewhere over the border
Is San Diego
But where has the ladder gone?

Grandfather Tells Time

Grandfather
Baseball cap insignia, faded
Gray sweater, no hood
Blue jeans worn from use
Granddaughter
Puffy pink jacket
Bouncy hair and crayons
Grandfather tells time
Granddaughter eats her fries
"Finish your food
At one, we'll go to the park
By two, we'll be on our way to your Mom's"
Grandfather tells time
Gray hairs cross his watch
Their time is short
He'll have to drop her off.

Grandfather folds his arms
Son is doing time
He misses this time
So quickly, she grows
Grandfather takes time for Granddaughter
Maple leaves in wind
Granddaughter never wants their afternoon walks
Her evening bike rides to end
Sometimes Grandfather tries to tell her about Son
About his time
She never listens
She hums and rides on

Says, "Watch me"
So, Grandfather does.

Son never got enough time from Grandfather
So much pain before he left
Grandfather was quiet during the arraignment
Hugged Grandmother as Son was taken
It all seemed to last so long.

In the fast food restaurant
Grandfather wonders why
Why it was not enough to provide
To wake up each dark morning and work
For his family
As Great Grandfather had done
Great Grandfather's sleep and silence in the evening
The silence of the open field
Within the cacophony of the worksite
Son never understood
That food was love
That working for your family was enough
Wasn't it?
Grandfather wishes he had more time to think about it.

Granddaughter's fries are done
So, Grandfather tells time
"Time to go to the park
Before I take you to your Mom's"
Granddaughter wants to stay
Motions over at some noisy kids
A collection of brightly-colored plastic balls

Says she wants to play
So, Grandfather lets her
Granddaughter jumps in
Makes quick friends
Tells them all to grab a bunch of balls
And throw them into the air
Like an explosion
Like fireworks
Like a scattered pile of leaves
Grandfather doesn't like this place
He feels out of place and contained
But he sits there in that plastic and metal chair
He takes time
He makes time
Looks at the time
Then pulls his sweater sleeve over his watch.

Flowers

Concierto de al-Andalus

A:00

African feet glide
Somewhere in the Maghreb
Through waving blades of green grass
And crunch
Darkness comes
Over a field in twilight
African children run
In joy and haste
Somewhere in the distance
A fire is built
Tongues of fire crackle over branches
Embers pop into blue and purple heavens
The children tease each other and laugh
The tall African man
With thick beard
Short hair
Black tawb
And black taqiyah
Stands before the flames
Awaiting the arrival of the children
They have come to hear a story
A story of the Imazighen
Of Africa
Of the Moors
Of al-Andalus
Spain.

A:55

The wind is a melody
Each breeze is a note
An African man
Aderfi
Stands atop a hill
In the distance is a small village
Aderfi closes his eyes
Feels the music curl around his fingers
He nods as it caresses his neck
The wind pulls his limbs into a lazy dance
He bows and offers up his hand as salutation
To a setting sun
A pile of gathered wood behind him sits waiting
A look of melancholy plays upon his face
He ceases his movements
Turns his back on the sun
Picks up his pile of wood
He whistles as he begins his journey home.

B:38

Aderfi's wife
Takama
Stands outside of their home
The wind catches the ends of the thatching
They wave like tiny flags
The edges of Takama's braided hair caught in the same breeze
She stands still
Dignified and impatient

Stares into the distance
Towards the waving hill
In her husband's direction
She waits for the wood to come
Suspects the night will grow cold
Inside their home
Their little children huddle together.

C:26

Through branches they look on
Towards the village
Colored keffiyehs
Brown and black skin tattooed
Inquisitive eyes
Whispers from dark bearded mouths to ears
The Moors point with bare and gloved hands.

C:40

The Imazighen
Gather in groups by fires outside
Preparing food
On tree branch skewers and in red clay pots
Gray water boiling
Imazighen move piles of wood into their homes
They work bow drills to start their fires
Older children play and are chased by adults inside.

C:58

The Moors adjust the swords in their sheathes
Robes and legs climb over the torsos of horses
Feet enter stirrups
They ride
Black hooves slice through tall green grass.

D:18

Imazighen see the robed men approaching
They yell silently
Most flee in terror
Moors unsheathe their swords
They are silhouettes of deadly intent
They strike down all Imazighen who stand
The hooves of their horses trample over them
Moors cast their nets
Towards the Imazighen who run
Dozens are caught
Men on the ground scream for their wives
Babies in the arms of robed men wail for their mothers
The Moors dismount from their horses
Their sandaled feet walk among Imazighen
The clenched hands of Moors hold rope
The Moors bind black hands and feet.

E:36

Aderfi watches in terror
From atop the hill
He drops his firewood
And runs down along the slope

In his haste he trips and tumbles down
Scraping skin
Exposing blood
Aderfi grits his teeth
He picks himself up
And continues to run.

F:03

The Moors
Tie the Imazighen from one to the other
The ends of the ropes to the mounts of their horses.

F:15

Aderfi creeps up to bushes
On the outskirts of the village
His eyes dart through the crowd
Moors off and on their horses
Pulling Imazighen by rope
Man and woman
Young and old
Some screaming
Some already walking with their heads lowered
Aderfi seethes with fury in the bushes
He searches for a rock he can use as a weapon.

F:28

A foot enters behind him
Aderfi turns in alarm

To see a net cast all around
He is caught and pulled
He yells and flails
A group of Moors descend upon him.

F:43

The Moors bind Aderfi's feet
The Moors tie him to a line of his people
The Moors lash him with their whips
The Moors gather the Imazighen
The Moors make them sit
The Moors eat the food from their tree branch skewers
And red clay pots
The Moors keep watch with quiet menace around the fire
The Moors pull the Imazighen up at dawn
The Moors march them across the grass
The Moors march them through the desert
The Moors march them to an encampment by the sea
The Moors separate the men from the women and children
The Moors pull them onto galleys
The Moors make the men take up oars
The galleys head out to sea.

G:35

The Imazighen have become slaves
The slaves are weather-wracked and tired
They row the ship
And row the ship
And row the ship

Looks of anger
Fear
Pain
Determination
And utter hopelessness
Play and stay upon the faces of each man
They row through the crashing waves of the Mediterranean.

H:21

Aderfi sits at an oar
Alongside four other men
They row
In a world of mist
Aderfi stares into the distance
He spots land as the fog slowly parts like a curtain
A large green mystical mountain
And on its sharp peak
A mighty Moorish castle with its turrets looms.

H:48

The galley pulls into a harbor
The slaves are untied and marched off
The Moors march them up a cobbled street
Into a town at the foot of the mountain
More soldiers and slaves arrive
They are Africans from the South
Arabs from the East
Normans, Gauls, and Celts from the North.

I:13

Bannermen and trumpeters herald the arrival of a general
The general rides his horse along the lines
He looks at the slaves
His eyes train upon them with disdain
He gives orders
His captains bark them back at the men
Each slave is passed a short sword
They are whipped and prodded into lines
Pointed forward
They become as one army on the march.

J:24

The army marches upon fields
Over hills
And through deserts
The soldiers march
As sunsets and sunrises dissolve into one another
Around campfires at night
The slaves train with their swords
The army gathers water into skins at the wells
The Moors stop to give their Salat wherever they go.

K:11

The army marches through a mountain pass
Of dirt and gray boulders
The soldiers drink from their skins
Beads of sweat tumble from their foreheads

A wind sweeps through the canyon kicking up dust
The horses neigh and buck
The soldiers raise their cloaks
The slaves raise their arms and squint their eyes in misery
One slave trips into another of a different tribe
A fight breaks out among them
But it is soon finished
As some are lost in the dust
And others continue marching through the canyon
The wind dies down
The army makes camp in the pass.

L:21

At night
Aderfi
Sits around a campfire
Looks at the trumpeters and the bannermen
Stares at a trumpet laid on the dirt
A Moor taps him on the shoulder
The Moor sits by him
Traces the name of Allah with his finger in the sand
Motions for Aderfi to do the same
Aderfi begins his first word in Arabic.

M:00

Attackers surround the next day
The army still marching through the mountain pass
The attackers are hidden behind boulders
They move slowly

Some crawl on their bellies
Closer and closer to their enemy
Escaping the army's notice
They give signals to each other as they lie in wait.

M:12

The attackers leap out from their concealment
They attack with daggers and strike down Moorish bannermen
The Moorish trumpeters begin to play
The general is knocked off his horse
The throats of Moorish soldiers are slit with crimson
A slave is stabbed through his chest.

M:34

Aderfi holds a short sword among the other slaves
A Moorish trumpeter is struck down near him
His trumpet rolls to the ground
Aderfi moves towards it
He picks it up and blows.

M:52

Soldiers and slaves move back into formation
They fight the attackers sword to dagger and win
Aderfi rides upon a horse galloping through the canyon
He sounds the trumpet
The men rally around his tune
They reform their lines
The remaining attackers flee into the rocks

The soldiers and slaves hold their weapons and pant
They are drenched in sweat and blood
Many lay scattered on the field
The army is victorious.

N:26

Aderfi is decorated by Abd al-Rahman
Emir of al-Andalus
In a ceremony in the great hall of the castle
Majestic banners hang
Trumpeters blare
Aderfi is dressed in fine military clothes
He wears a keffiyeh on his head
Stands in a line of soldiers and slaves
Presented with gifts and medals by their general
Aderfi is given a trumpet.

O:08

Aderfi walks in his fine military clothes
Trumpet in hand
He walks under Moorish arches
Through the palace gardens under gray skies by fountains
His hands dip into the pools
Caress the petals of Valencia roses
Aderfi sees a set of steps and a path up to one of the turrets
He climbs the steps with his trumpet in hand
The turret balcony is empty
The wind blows through Aderfi's keffiyeh and clothes
He raises his trumpet to his lips and begins to play.

0:46

Aderfi's tune is the mountain pass where bodies still lay
His tune is the waves of the Mediterranean
His tune is the birds in the sky over the sea
His tune is the port where Takama and their children
Were boarded onto a separate ship
His tune is Takama and their children in their home in Africa
His tune is making love to Takama there.

P:18

Aderfi stops playing atop the turret of the castle
He hangs his head
Pulls down his keffiyeh
Tears stream down his face.

P:31

Aderfi looks out back towards the turret stairs
Takama is standing there
On the tower balcony
She wears a black niqab
Her eyes glisten
They stare at each other for long moments
They are as ghosts to each other
Doubtful of the other's existence.

P:44

Aderfi and Takama hold each other for the first time in years
The wind blows through Aderfi's hair and Takama's hijab
Takama weeps as they continue their embrace
On the turret
Of the castle
On the peak
Of the land
That is al-Andalus.

Q:09

In Africa
Somwhere in the Maghreb
Tongues of fire still crackle over branches
As embers pop into blue and purple heavens.

Mountain Meadows

The walls of the chapel
Bear no cross
By the pews
In blue bonnets
The saints walk
Scattered in different families
Seventeen children join the lines
In Utah Territory
It is the year of our Lord
1859.

Learn you well
About Brigham Young
And the Teachings of the Prophet Joseph Smith
These young ones are raised in faith
Family
And in discipline
Some are raised in love
After two years
They have become the community's own
But upon plains and meadows
And sometimes in chapel
Fathers still avoid looking the older children in the eye
And the whispers of their mothers by woodfire
Carry through the night.

These seventeen
Know they don't belong
Although some of them have forgotten to care

They dream now of low grasses and of red rocks
In place of the lush greens of the Ozarks
They dream now of valleys and hills
Instead of rivers and deltas
They pray with their families
They play with their toys and their friends.

Others
They remember
Their fathers and mothers
Faces
Clothes
And temperaments
Different
A whole wagon train of
Uncles
Aunts
And cousins
Bosses and hands
Moving
The steady sight of white canvas
An arch
Over their heads
In sun
Rain
Sleet
And in snow
They remember the neighing of the horses
And the familiar stink of the cattle
They remember
Father's rough hands

And mother's smooth cross
The one that hung from her neck
The one that has been gone.

Screams
Sobbing
Gunfire
Running feet
The glint of the sun
On the edge of a bow knife
Blinding
Skin loose
White men dressed as Paiutes
Faces frozen
Others utterly scared
The men
Women and children
Separated from each other
Led to march in different directions
A white flag
Their mother's scalp
Bloody
On the ground.

Those who remember
They remember it in their nightmares
Or when they stare off too long into the horizon
Or when they watch the wind blow through the grass
Or when everything goes quiet
Or when the priest speaks of Hell.
Those who remember

They keep time
In the trunks of trees
The walls of houses
In the patterns they knit
In the pages of scripture
It has been
Almost two years.

Those who remember
In different ways
They know
It wasn't all that far from where they live now.

The bodies of those they loved
Were left to rot in an open field
As the seventeen children were taken away
And left to live with other fathers
Other mothers
And other siblings.

Some other fathers still had blood soaked into their sleeves
When they brought the children into their homes.

In 1859
Other fathers are crying
Other mothers are angry
Other siblings are unsure of what is happening
A man named Jacob Forney has come
To take the seventeen back to Arkansas.

They leave quickly

In wagons and on trains the seventeen children ride
Some things
Across the country
And in the land of their ancestors
Are familiar sights
For some
Marion
Crawford
Carroll
And Johnson
Are home sweet home
But some of those children will always live in Utah
And some of them will never leave
Mountain Meadows.

Lili'uokalani

For Tim Broad

December 31st, 1895

Dearest Brother,

I hope all is well with you in Cambridge
This time of year
I cannot say I miss Massachusetts
I write to you
From the summery island of O'ahu
It is unfortunately
Under gloomy circumstances.

As you may have surmised
I am in an ongoing battle with the papers on the islands
The Republicans
Tirelessly defending
Their upstart Republic of Hawaii
I continue
Steadfast
On the side of the native people
And their unjustly imprisoned monarch
Queen Lili'uokalani
(With whom I continue to communicate
Through a number of intermediaries).

In your last letter
You fancied Her Majesty a Rapunzel
A fairy tale princess imprisoned in a castle

Trying to write and sing her way out of her captivity
To reclaim her nation of islands with ink and paper
Would you say these many letters she is writing
These dozens of golden songs she is composing
Be the strands of hair she is letting down from the Royal Palace?
While I confess to being utterly tangled up in all of it, now
I must beg to differ, my brother
That girl Rapunzel was imprisoned by a crone in a tower
Deep into the woods
Queen Lili'uokalani is imprisoned in plain sight
In Honolulu
The capital
'Iolani Palace
The seat of power of her people for generations.

The Queen is more like your friend Odysseus
Rightful ruler of Ithaca
Returned to claim his throne
Only to find it filled with scoundrels and sycophants
Penelope, the islands of Hawai'i
Her Majesty brought to a palace most recently occupied
By the self-appointed President Sanford B. Dole
And some of the very men
The Queen, herself, had appointed into office!
And how kind of them to restore her, to 'Iolani!

Your Odysseus had only one Telemachus
Loyal sons of Hawai'i
Queen Lili'uokalani
Had two
Whose lives were threatened by the rope

To save them
She abdicated the throne
Unlike Odysseus
The traitors found the bow of the Queen
Before she could use it
Her Majesty had fought against the Republicans
While in power
And, before that, during the reign of her brother
King Kalākaua
So, why not continue to fight the conspirators
After they had disposed of the Kingdom?
And now
To the shame of her nation
ʻIolani Palace
Converted into Her Majesty's prison
Unlike Odysseus
Her Majesty must string her bow again
With her letters on paper
With the notes she writes
With the songs she sings
With the instruments she can only imagine playing.

In my last letter
I told you Her Majesty's name
Liliʻuokalani
Was translated in the literal sense to,
"Smarting of the Royal Ones"
And now I know why
Her birth name
Liliʻu Loloku Walania Kamakaʻeha
Was composed of four Hawaiian words

Liliʻu (smarting)
Loloku (tearful)
Walania (a burning pain)
Kamakaʻeha (sore eyes)
Her Majesty was named by
The regent Elizabeth Kīnaʻu
Who had an eye infection at the time
And while it may seem odd to us
It is Hawaiian custom
To name a child to an event linked to their birth.

To the matter of the Queen
Currently being "tearful"
Or having "sore eyes"
Nearly all I have heard tell
Through correspondences
With Her Majesty's lady-in-waiting
Mrs. Eveline Townsend Wilson
(Or "Kitty," as she affectionately likes to be called)
Is that the Queen is always in good spirits
Always brandishes a smile
Or, keeps a strong face
That even when she writes and sings
Of the most tearful of goodbyes
To lovers long gone
Her Majesty never shows that pain to the world.

Brother George,
I have told you
Of the most heinous betrayal
Suffered by Queen Liliʻuokalani

At the hands of the conspirators
And have alluded to Odysseus
And his vengeance
And yet
Her Majesty's heart
Is filled with the most Christian of forgiveness.

I once asked Her Majesty in a letter
(After she had entrusted me with
One of her latest compositions),
"How can you write songs of such love
Songs proclaiming the glory of God
Of His infinite wisdom and mercy
And, of your nation
Of these sunny sea girt isles
Of rain-swept cliffs
The bright red spindles of the ʻāhihi lehua
The Kipuʻu rain of the forest
And the bird's lehua nectar?
How can Your Grace write all of this
Whilst staring out a few scant windows?"

Queen Liliʻuokalani wrote back in reply,
"My dear Captain Palmer,
Every poem that has ever been written
And tune that has ever been composed
Has been done so
In captivity
Just as our eternal souls
Are imprisoned in this flesh
And released by God

So, too, are our hearts captive
Only to be released in song."

Her Majesty continued,
With her lauded wit,
"Captain Palmer,
You ask me
While imprisoned
Without a kingdom to rule
How I can write these songs
Truth be told
I do not know
As it terribly complicates my otherwise full
Schedule of official State visits and social engagements."

In spite of myself
I chortled as I read that
All the while knowing
Her Majesty's room was small
Her doors were locked
Her only visitors
Mrs. Wilcox
And her tormentors.

And yet she writes
And yet she sings.

So, I tell you
Dear brother
It is not Queen Liliʻuokalani
Who is imprisoned

It is we
We who are held captive by our secrets
By the weaknesses of our bodies
By the things we hold onto
Both material and immaterial
It is we who are chained
To the possessions we covet
Our unyielding craving for more
It is we who are caged in the bars
Of our fear and our pride.

This is one
Of the many things
I have learned
From Queen Liliʻuokalani.

I do not know when
Her Majesty will be released
I do not know if
The Queen will ever return
To the United States of America
To plead her case for the restoration of her throne
And the sovereignty of her people
But I know in my heart
That her songs will make it to our shores someday
I dare say
They will live on and be remembered
For as long as a single flame burns at the center of Kilauea.

Until we meet again
Dear brother.

Aloha (good day, fare thee well).

Sincerely,

Julius A. Palmer, Jr.
Sea Captain
Writer, *Evening Post*

Beloved

Secret Beaches

Secret beaches
Tend not to live up to their name
Though they often mean a lot
To those who name them
"Secret"
Today we walk your secret beach together
The meaning is not lost on me
Today we walk your secret beach together
Like mad and innocent children
You make me feel ancient
We have a history
Years ago, I took you to a secret beach
Where we shared our first kiss
Under a shining sun
The crashing of waves as our soundtrack
You've brought me here
So that I could hear it playing again
Irresistible, I pull you towards me once more
Like the surf falling from the seashore
This all feels inevitable
Our lips and our tongues finally part ways
I look into your face
No longer seeing the woman you have become
But the girl you once were
The girl I once found
The sweet princess
With a heart surrounded by razor blades
A sandcastle protected by landmines
You had placed them there yourself

Part sadism
Part masochism
Cynicism and sarcasm
I loved it all
I love to see you smile
You are mine again
It's like you never left
The secret beach is playing our soundtrack
But it keeps on skipping on this track
With thoughts of tears
And father
And pity
Tears
Father
Pity
He said to me,
"Son, I never want to see you like this again"
Again and again
In my memory
My friends come up a hill
Something in their slow approach
Highly suggestive
Heavy
Burdened with bad news
Unfaithful
Unfaithful
You stand upon this beach
Asking for forgiveness
When you don't have anything nice to say
YOU shouldn't say anything at all
So, I am silent

Your smile is beautiful
Vulnerable and open
My smile is here too
Closed
Impatient
Full of hate
We have a history
You are comfortable in my arms
A girl I once found
A woman who would be mine
Part sadism
Part masochism
Cynicism and sarcasm
I loved it all
As I love the beach
I will never love you again
Will never believe in secret beaches again
You are not a girl any longer
You are a woman
I am a man
Secrets are not kept
Others will walk upon this beach.

The Woman with Many Names

I will call you my wild woman
Because you curse like a sailor
And stand tall like a pin-up
I leave skin deep for
Men on leave
And the tourists
Me?
I'm anchored to your hip bone
There, I play Morse code
And call you,
"My poppyseed"
I will call you gypsy
With hair full of skulls and skeletons
So dark and deep
A web of intrigue
I will call you brilliant
As you catch the moonlight
Skin as fair as vanilla white
I will call you Catwoman
When I hear your soft steps
And notice those black clothes
Clinging tight to all the right curves
I will call you glamorous
The one mistaken for a silent film actress
I will call you painter
When your acrylic and ink
Speaks louder than any crowd
I will make moves to seduce you
In the antique room

With bravado and parlor tricks
It will be you who will convince me
With the help of gold leaf
That you have descended from Mexican oil money
And a long line of proud 18th century rabbits
I'll believe you
Because it's evident from our smoking gums
That we share some of the same bad habits
I couldn't be happier
If I had saved you from being sawn in half
Or pulled you like magic from my hat
I will call you my partner
Because you refuse to just stand there
And play quiet girlfriend
I will call you my partner
Because you are
My boss
Camera crew
Producer and director
In the field or in private
We say "action" to each other
And always move on cue
I will call you my partner
Because you're delightful as…
And you keep it that way
I want to see you every day
I will call you many things
What could you call the woman with so many names?
I will call you
The woman of my nights
And my mornings

I will call you
My…

It Could've Been Magic

It started well enough
A dusty old road
In a small and quiet town
A loud-talking rabbit
Carrying a banjo
And a doctor's black case
She was yelling at cars
Giving the finger
To the passersby
By the roadside
She met a mild-mannered magician
With more holes in his pockets
Than tricks up his sleeves
The magician walked up
Kicking up dust
In cheap brown shoes
Red handkerchief in hand
He stammered
And yammered
He talked
He made that bunny blush
And the loud-talking rabbit
Between cigs
Between gigs
Between cities
Who was looking to hitch-hike
Her way back
Over to the next county
Put her thumb down

For a moment
The magician removed his top hat
He asked her
"I don't mean to come off rude
But I'm looking for a rabbit
To pull out of my hat
And I think you'd be perfect for my act!"
She said,
"That might be fine
Because I'm a banjo player
And I will strum these strings
In front of five
Or five thousand
I'll tell you what
You line up the gigs for us
If you don't mind doing a double act
I'll be your bunny in a hat!"
The magician and the rabbit
They agreed to work together
And continued down that road together
But together isn't forever.

They opened with magic
Closed with music
The bunny was no stranger to show business
But new to the prestige
She was a natural
Cramped herself into
Hidden hat compartments
Crawled up the magician's sleeves
Knew how to make a grand entrance

Or when to stall for time
Knew when to make her final bows
Gracious
Or filled with swagger
And after their magic shows had ended
And they had parted the curtain
To the sound of applause
The magician removed his coat
Remarked how
They'd "had another great show"
Said he'd,
"Never been happier"
The rabbit nodded
Then picked up her banjo
Pulled open that curtain
And walked back onto the stage
She played
Blues songs
Mostly covers
Filled with twangs
Claw strums
And gallows humor
Sometimes she admitted
Even she didn't get it
But her following was strong
And it grew
Sometimes before shows
They would talk of tours
Booking agents
And promoters
Carnival tents

Back alley bars
And majestic concert halls
Each night
They slept
In cheap motels
Barnyards
Or in alleys
Leaning up against
Cold and unforgiving
Dumpsters
Sometimes they would cuddle up
In the magician's tattered black coat
Looking up through narrow slits
Between buildings
At the stars
The rabbit would say,
"If I could have anything
It would be a place in the big city
Some place
To finally
Set down my bags
Hang up my banjo
And just be
Home...
You see
I've never had one."
The magician nodded
Like he understood
What she meant
How she felt
But he didn't

He just held her
Until dawn
The rabbit asked
If the magician could find any bigger events
Or venues for them to play around town
He said he couldn't
Because there weren't any
Or they were all pay to play
And he was still substituting
Pennies
For silver dollars behind ears
The magician was finally learning
Something about saving money
In mason jars
Versus making it disappear
But neither the gigs
Nor the money were pouring in
And night after night
The rabbit and the magician
Found themselves back in the alleys
The magician and the rabbit performed together
But together isn't forever.

So, when the rabbit asked him
If he was fine with her going solo
He said
That he too
Could benefit from doing shows on his own
Illusions were
After all
Beautifully crafted lies

And creating and performing illusions
Was a magician's calling.

Then one day
The rabbit returned from a gig
At dawn
With her banjo
And doctor's black case in hand
Looking and acting a bit different
She said,
"I've found an ongoing gig in the city"
The magician suddenly felt queasy
She said,
"I'm leaving…
This morning"
The magician shuffled his feet
And removed his top hat
He replied,
"That's great
I'm really happy for you"
She smiled and said,
"It's been a pleasure working with you"
"Same here,"
He answered
She picked up her banjo
And her doctor's black case
The magician asked,
"Will you find your home
In that big city?"
She answered,
"I hope so"

"Do you still love playing?"
He asked
She patted her banjo,
"Yes
I do,"
"I'm glad,"
He said
They shook hands
"Goodbye"
"Goodbye"
She turned and walked to the roadside
The magician watched her walk
For about a quarter of a mile
Tears were soaked
Into his red handkerchief
And tattered black coat sleeve
The magician waved his magic wand
Over his top hat…
But the rabbit remained in the distance
His hat
Held no rabbit inside
He yelled out
Wistfully towards her,
"It could've been magic!"
The rabbit turned for a moment
Yelled back,
"It was!"

And the rabbit left for the city to start her new life.

Rosemary

My father called for you
On deathbed
Through murmured words
I had wondered what requests he would have
But you were the only one
"Where is my Rosemary?"
I didn't expect you to come
You arrived that December
We didn't talk much
Stared at him sleeping
Sat with my family
Made small talk
Then we caught up alone outside
Those moments
Fit between kind gesture
And the type of thing you keep with you forever
Hand in hand on the couch
Hinting at something we had never truly had
A hug tight in the cold
And then a question,
"Do you need anything Romero?"
That's what you called me
That and "Rosemary"
Because you knew how proud I was
How proud of my name
How foolish a Mexican
Who didn't speak Spanish
Who hadn't known "Romero"
Didn't mean something dangerous or manly

Or any of the vague concepts
He had made it out to be
I would groan in disgust and disbelief
With thoughts of that delicate herb
"Rosemary!"
You would laugh with glee
Sprint with impossibly long hair let down
My Titania
My Rosemary
That name was yours if you had wanted it
When you came back that December
You did not laugh
Your hair was short
A face I knew
Years older
A weighted cheek
Eyes filled with concern
I lingered on that look
The outcome was bleak
There was longing in that reflection
But it was probably all mine.

Etymology

Our Name Is Romero

We are artists
Nuns
Laborers
Managers and supervisors
Workers and entrepreneurs
Housewives and mothers
We are alive
And we are buried
We tend to our name
Yearly
We tend to these stones
As my father had done
Our name is Romero.

Our name is Romero
Like Frank Romero
From Lanfranco Street
To Los Four in New York
And beyond
Romero like Sonia Romero
Installations on the Metro
And She Rides the Lion Studio.

Our land was Romero
In New Mexico / Nuevo México
Until quills touched upon papers
Land deeds in Agua Fria
Made worthless in moments
Most cross the border

The border crossed us.

My grandfather Edward
Born in New Mexico
The fifth child
Of my great grandmother
Donaciana
Quickly passed away
My great grandfather
Emiterio
Quickly remarried
Edward's aunt Connie raised him
They left New Mexico
Moved to California
Three brothers
In name and blood
Came from Edward
Frank
Richard
And Gerard.
We came from Richard.

Our name is Romero
We are pochxs
Chicanxs
Whitewashed
Non-Spanish-speaking
Mexican-Americans
First
Second
Third

Fourth
Fifth generation
Most do not understand
What it is to have come from a state
That was once Mexico
And before?
The Viceroyalty of New Spain
And before that?

España
A man of La Mancha
Bartolome II
Often confused as the first of his name
A man most likely poor
The first Romero
Of our line
To touch ground
Upon the shores of The New World.

The Expedition of Oñate
"The Last Great Conquistador"
Ordered pueblo natives made slaves
Ordered pueblo natives killed
Ordered pueblo natives' legs removed
As punishment for their insurrection
Captain Bartolome Romero was a butcher
He had to have been
Under Oñate
Romero
Was promoted to captain from the rank of ensign.

This Bartolome
This Romero
He is a part of us
He gave us our name.

What follows
Is what we make.

We tend to our name
Yearly
We tend to these stones
With my father's burlap bag
Filled with his rusty tools
We cut the grass around these stones
Find the hole
Dig our fingers into the dirt
Fill the black metal vase with water
Place in freshly-bought flowers
We do this
As our father had done
Remember those who have come before
Those we know
And those lost to history
Our name is Romero.

My Name Is Romero Discussion Guide

Undocumented Football

"Miguel's too fast though. How fast? Too fast. Too fast for borders, laws, checkpoints, dogs. Too fast for fences, ditches, detention centers, and walls."

What are some stereotypes surrounding border crossing? Are all Latinx people in the US people who have crossed the Mexico-United States border?

"Miguel never cared for politics. He just loved his coach, his team, this American game of football. His dream: to make a catch in the only important game that he could."

Miguel is a fictional character, but he is based on the real-life un-docuqueer activist Isaac Barrera, a record-setting running back at Belmont High School. Latinx people are known for loving fútbol/soccer, but also play a wide variety of sports in the US and throughout Latin America. When Latinx-Americans take interest in other cultures, through activities like sports or music, does doing so make them any less Latinx?

"There are so many reasons to drop the ball. Walk out of this stadium just a statistic; undocumented student, faceless immigrant."

"The model minority" stereotype puts pressure on undocumented immigrants to excel in society. Why is expecting immigrants to "prove their worth" problematic?

Make Me More Mexican

"Hold your tongue. Do not think to criticize me for speaking English, when you, too, so proudly speak the language of your European rapists, murderers, and conquerors: Spanish."

Do all Latinx people speak Spanish? Does not speaking Spanish make Latinx people, especially Mexican-Americans, less Latinx and less Mexican?

Why do so many Latinx people have a strong connection to the Spanish language? How do Spanish dialects vary among Latinx Americans? Can these dialects reflect indigenous languages as well as interaction with other non-Latinx cultures, such as with Africans, Asians, and others?

"Make me more Mexican... I heard they were performing the procedure somewhere in a dilapidated warehouse somewhere in Tijuana. It involves infusions of chile, gargling mole, consuming peyote infused Chiclets, classes on how to sell oranges."

Are poverty, and an association with criminal activities, negative stereotypes that affect Latinxs? Is it possible to present stereotypes in a piece of art in order to deconstruct them? Can presenting negative stereotypes, even with good intentions, do more harm than good?

"Be priests, architects, and presidents! Cops and convicts! Sinners and saints!"

Latinx people have been stereotyped as both unruly menaces to society (either as drunks, criminals, or political dissidents) and as quiet people, who value faith and family, and mostly keep to themselves. What are the limits of each stereotype? Are members of any ethnic group merely one way or the other? How does presenting a spectrum of identity free people to be themselves?

Gorilla Arms

"No one had ever told me I should want to be like my father. Blue-collar. Work with your hands."

Do all Latinx-Americans work blue collar jobs? What are some white collar jobs Latinx-Americans occupy? What are some stereotypes surrounding Latinx blue collar workers?

"You look like a gorilla.' There was hate there. Disgust there. Dehumanization."

What are some of the stereotypes surrounding ethnic groups that have likened them to animals? How has dehumanization been used throughout history to facilitate racism and oppression?

Have you ever judged a person of Latinx descent based upon a stereotype? Have you ever judged a friend or family member based upon a stereotype?

Micro Machines

"There's a dusty wood and tin garage under this museum and the docent has put his uncle into it. They call this aggression, but, really, it's so easy, as she does it."

"Micro Machines" is a poem about a microaggression said to Romero at a young age about his uncle. A microaggression is a statement, action, or incident regarded as an instance of indirect, subtle, or unintentional discrimination against members of a marginalized group. Are most experiences with racism confrontational or violent, or are they microaggressions? When someone expresses a microaggression towards us, do we always take the time to let them know that it's not ok? How can being silent in the face of microaggressions affect the way we see ourselves and others?

"There is nothing wrong with painting cars, painting pictures of cars, or, dressing like a cholo. But, we are not all the same. You can't paint us all with the same brush. Fit us all into the same stroke. Whatever the medium, there is nothing wrong with taking pride in your work. But, what is wrong is for anyone to assume that we are a smaller people; a lesser people."

Negative stereotypes towards Latinx often portray us as being uneducated and uncultured. What are some of the ways Latinx people have represented themselves in art, dance, theater, music, literature, and film?

Open Letter to Donald Trump

"You called us criminals, drug dealers, and rapists."

How did Donald Trump's campaign speech play into the worst Latinx stereotypes? What are some of the positive contributions that Latinx people, specifically immigrants, make to the US?

> *"A nameless wave of people from Mexico and South America. Donald Trump have you heard of Central America? Thought to throw in a statistic? Like 7% of immigrants come to the US from El Salvador, Guatemala, and Honduras. Would saying the places we come from, the most basic of differences, have alienated your supporters?"*

Why do Americans of various backgrounds tend to think of Latinx Americans as all being Mexican? Some Latinx-Americans have chosen to believe that Trump was not also talking about them in his speech. What are some of the antagonisms between Mexicans and other Latinx people? Is anti-immigrant sentiment in the US related to racist sentiment against Latinxs in general?

> *"We're the best of the best. The majority shareholders: in 2044, or earlier."*

People of color will make up over 50% of the US population by the year 2044. Latinx Americans will make up over a quarter of the US population around the same time. How could the continued growth of the Latinx American population shape the US; politically, economically, and culturally?

Acknowledgements

First off, I'd like to thank the many members of my family: from my siblings Julie, Kathleen, and Matt, to my mother Carmen, to my nieces Felicia, Kaelyn, and Larissa, to my many cousins: Jurados, Perezes, Alcalas, Floreses, Durans, Silvas, Altamiranos, Arriolas, Ramirezes, Salgados, Melendrezes, Holguins, Lopezes, and many more, who have loved and supported me through the years. Specific names that I must give credit to, who were especially helpful in genealogical research, are Tom Jurado, Frank Ramirez, and the late Antoinette Silva. While I did not choose to include the material they provided in this book, it was all foundational in the drive to write it, and I do intend to create a record that will contain all of that genealogical research for the private use of our families.

I'd like to thank those dozens of administrators, professors, department chairs, and students who have brought me to perform, present, and/or lead workshops on their campuses. Toi Thibodeaux and Lorena Marquez, specifically, have been instrumental in helping me build a career as a writer, performer, and speaker.

I'd like to thank my publisher, Edward Vidaurre, Editor-in-chief of FlowerSong Press, for choosing to publish this manuscript and for supporting me every step of the way. It is an honor to be listed among so many gifted emerging and established writers in Texas, California, and beyond, with FlowerSong Press.

Thank you to my best friend in poetry, Matt Sedillo, for recommending that I reach out to Edward Vidaurre and FlowerSong Press. Without Sedillo, this wouldn't have been possible. Thank you for being my friend, and my closest rival. When you race, I race. Let's see who gets left behind.

I'd like to thank Gustavo Arellano, Curtis Marez, Ulises Bella, Yolanda Nieves, Mike "The Poet" Sonksen, and Ana Maria Alvarez for their advance reviews of the book.

I'd like to thank some of the other poets who continue to inspire me (listed roughly, in the order in which I met them): Saul Williams, Mayda del Valle, Beau Sia, Mark Gonzalez, Gabriela Garcia Medina, Poetri, Shihan, Traci Kato-kiriyama, Alvin Lau, Jon Sands, Paul Mabon, IN-Q, Tshaka Campbell, Nikki Blak, Besskepp, Simply Kat, Treesje Thomas, Judah1, SuperB, MC Prototype, Mark Lipman, Ant Black, Rudy Francisco, Shelley Bruce, Luis J. Rodriguez, Abel Salas, Mr. Poetic, John Martinez, Seth Walker, Mark Maza, Steady, Tyrone Stokes, Yesika Salgado, Angela Aguirre, Fisseha Moges, Myron Woods, Daniel Hees, and Denice Frohman. Some of the poets I have listed I have been fortunate enough to call friends, and others, I have only had the pleasure of meeting once or twice. To the thousands of other poets I have met, thank you too.

I'd like to thank my ex-girlfriends, their families, and their friends: for their affection and wisdom, for their kindness to welcome me into their homes and/or to take me on trips, and, in some cases, I thank them for their forgiveness.

I would especially like to thank my late brother-in-law Tim Broad. Tim was a husband, father and grandfather. He was also a deputy sheriff for thirty years. Tim enjoyed golfing, listening to Hawaiian music and playing the guitar. He had a black belt in Kenpo Karate and jiu-jitsu.

Tim would routinely ask me how my touring was going and if I was working on anything new, creatively. That was special. I do not begrudge family members and friends for not taking more interest in these things, but it meant a lot that Tim was always interested. He was like an older brother to me, an uncle, or a friend. His slack key guitar playing, even as a private hobby for him, gave us something in common, we were both creative. He even began to teach me a couple of tunes. Tim came from a family of entertainers. News of his passing, and the many feelings it stirred up, hurt. There was a lot of pain and anger. Eventually, reflecting on Tim's life and death, was an impetus to finish this manuscript; one I had been working on for nearly ten years.

It would have been much better for that not to have been the case. It would've been much better had Tim gotten a chance to read "Lili'uo-kalani," the poem he had asked me to write, but I didn't write until after his passing (as a Hawaiian, he felt connected to the story of the Queen and even casually supported Hawaiian independence).

More importantly, it would've been much better if Tim had lived to see his daughters and grandchildren grow up. I wish he could've continued to be a part of their lives.

It would've been much better if Tim and I had gone on that tour we often joked about, the one where he would play slack key guitar and I would perform poetry. Forget colleges, he said the first stop of our world tour would be inside a volcano! In his dad joke words, it was "gonna be explosive!"

Thank you, Tim. We'll miss you.

About the author

David A. Romero is a Mexican-American spoken word artist from Diamond Bar, CA. Romero has appeared at over 75 colleges and universities in over 30 different states in the USA. Romero was the second poet to be featured on All Def Digital. Romero has opened for Latin Grammy winning bands Ozomatli and La Santa Cecilia. Romero's work has been published alongside poets laureate Luis J. Rodriguez, Jack Hirschman, Alejandro Murguia, and Lawrence Ferlinghetti. Romero has won the Uptown Slam at the historic Green Mill in Chicago; the birthplace of slam poetry. Romero has appeared in-studio numerous times on multiple programs on KPFK 90.7 FM Los Angeles. Romero's poetry deals with family, identity, social justice issues, and Latinx culture.

Romero donates a percentage of funds earned from his collegiate engagements to various nonprofits and social justice organizations. Fall 2017 saw the launch of a scholarship for high school seniors who are interested in spoken word and social justice: "The Romero Scholarship for Excellence in Spoken Word." The first scholarship was awarded in 2018.

David A. Romero has received honorariums from: Arizona State University, The University of Utah, University of Missouri, Washington State University, The University of Memphis, Loyola University Chicago, University of Central Florida, USC, UCLA, and more!

Romero is a graduate of the University of Southern California, a double major in Film and Philosophy. Romero is the former host of Between the Bars Open Mic at the dba256 Gallery Wine Bar in Pomona, CA. Visit his website, www.davidaromero.com for more.

About the artist

Sonia Romero is a Los Angeles artist known for her paper-cut and printmaking aesthetics which she incorporates into both her fine art and public art commissions. Born in 1980, she grew up in an artistic household in Echo Park before formally studying at the Rhode Island School of Design. After returning to California, she began working as a public artist, and was the artist in residence at Avenue 50 Studio in Northeast Los Angeles from 2007-2014.

Calling upon her own experiences and perspectives as a multiracial person, Romero creates work that reflects the cultural diversity found in the communities of Los Angeles. She explores themes relating to the universal connectedness within humanity as well as its relationship to the environment. Her signature style, a dynamic combination of printmaking, paper-cutting, painting, and sculpture, includes fine art pieces that have been showcased in many galleries and acquired into the collections of prominent institutions such as the Los Angeles County Museum of Art and the Smithsonian. Her distinctive paper-cut shapes and patterns can be found in steel, tile, or paint in one of her many large-scale permanent installations in notable locations such as Little Tokyo, the Mariachi Plaza and MacArthur Park Metro Stations and the Artesia County Public Library.

soniaromero.net

Services

Performances

Looking for a poet to be a featured performer for your slam or open mic with a performance of around 30 minutes? Romero can also perform solo for a period up to 2 hours, entertaining your student body with his poems, stories, and slideshow featuring personal photographs as well as images from history and current events.

Workshops

Looking for a workshop leader to engage students to write about the issues that matter and the issues that matter to them? Romero leads workshops that teach writing techniques and performance skills, promote critical thinking around social issues, encourage attendees to open themselves up emotionally, and learn how to set goals and how to achieve them.

Presentations

Looking for a unique speaker who will present social justice issues in a way that is both challenging for the expert and immediately engaging for the novice? For audiences who would like to explore certain issues in greater depth than would be addressed in a performance, and would prefer to forego the interactivity of a workshop, Romero's presentations will educate, entertain, and inspire.

Please visit www.davidaromero.com for more.